what every JEHOVAH'S WITNESS should know

By Arthur M. Bowser

ACCENT BOOKS
Denver, Colorado

This Micro-Book brings into sharp focus topics of special interest within a theme of vital importance.

Copyright © 1975, 1976, 1978
Accent Publications, Inc.
Printed in U.S.A.
Eighth Printing

ACCENT BOOKS
Accent Publications, Inc.
P.O. Box 15337
Denver, Colorado 80215

CONTENTS

Jehovah—Mathematical Unity or Tri-Personality?/4

Man—Eternal or Temporal?/23

Satan—Presently Cast Down or Prospectively Cast Down?/48

Jesus—Deity or Deputy?/56

Jehovah -- Mathematical Unity or Tri-Personality?

My search ended one morning at 2 a.m. For days I had been poring over your Jehovah's Witnesses' publications to discover the answers to three questions: 1) What do you actually believe? 2) What foundational truths do you hold in common with those whom I call born-again believers? 3) Why does your teaching differ so markedly from what I and so many others believe?

Let me begin by answering the second question. It came as a surprise to discover that you Jehovah's Witnesses consider as basic a number of important Bible truths.

You believe that the Bible is the uniquely inspired Word of God. To quote one of your writers, "The Bible is Jehovah God's written word to mankind, revealing himself and expressing his purposes." You teach that the 66 books comprising the Scriptures contain the complete and sole message of salvation. You believe in the actual fulfillment of Biblical prophecy and divide Bible history into distinct dispensations. You view the Biblical revelation as an epic drama of world redemption in vindication of God's name, truth and purposes. You maintain that God is a spirit and through His Son Jesus is the immediate creator of all things. You oppose the evolutionary theory which insists that higher life developed from lower organisms. You consider Adam and Eve to be historical persons who originally imaged their Creator's attributes. You believe that Adam was put on probation in a literal garden of Eden which became the scene of the first sin. You teach that as a result of Adam's sin, all men experience physical death. You see Satan as the tempter of man and the bitter opponent of Jehovah through the ages. You declare that the "seed of woman" who will crush the devil is Jesus Christ. You are convinced that the preexisting Jesus became the Second Adam by the virgin birth. You stress His obedient life and necessary death on Calvary's "tree" as a ransom price. You affirm that God uniquely raised Jesus from the dead. You believe that this same Jesus, coming as a warrior-king, will oust Satan from the earth and will reign for a thousand years as Prince of Peace. You anticipate sharing in the perfections of the millennial kingdom.

After reading this list of tenets, the casual observer might conclude that your group's teaching is only a negligible variant of the historic Christian faith. However, an in-depth study reveals many basic differences.

According to your teaching, the God who created the earth is a unitary being whose exclusive personal identifying name is Jehovah and who is the Great Theocrat. This Jehovah is in no sense a trinity of persons but is the solitary supreme sovereign of the universe.

According to your views Jesus Christ, "the second greatest Personage of the universe" was the only being created directly by Jehovah and because of this He is called the only begotten Son. Using Jesus as His Chief Agent, Jehovah then brought all other things into existence. After Jesus, His mighty spirit creature, proved Himself faultless in the heavens, Jehovah appointed Him "as his Vindicator and Chief Agent of life toward mankind."

Since you deny that Christ is God, you necessarily deny his incarnation. You teach that the virgin birth was necessary so that Christ could be born as the perfect second Adam. Unlike the human Adam, however, the human Jesus in His earthly life proved sinless under test. You affirm that the death of the man Jesus was a human ransom in behalf of Adam's fallen children, guaranteeing them "another opportunity or trial for life everlasting." You insist this does not mean that Jesus is a personal Saviour from sin but that His death gives the worthy members of Adam's race the right to earn eternal life which they lost through the first man's sin.

You believe further that after three days in the grave, Jehovah raised Jesus as a spirit creature and that after forty days He ascended into Heaven to offer His sacrifice to Jehovah. What happened to the human body of Jesus? You surmise that it may be preserved somewhere for future exhibition during the Millennial Age. Of one thing you are certain, Jesus did not rise physically in a human body because that would somehow mean that He was taking back the ransom price.

Your teaching is quick to point out that the "holy spirit" is not a person, much less a person of the Godhead, but is instead "Jehovah's invisible energizing force that produces visible results in many manifestations experienced by men."

Man, according to your teaching, is similar to the animals in that he does not possess an immortal soul distinct from the body but *is* an earthly soul or organism of flesh kept alive by the circulation of blood. Man, the human soul, was created only for the earth and by obedience to Jehovah can earn the right to live forever on the future restored earthly Paradise.

Because Adam sinned "by refusing to hold to God's High Standard of Glory" human physical death comes upon all men. You claim that death is the utter cessation of all conscious activity and "the termination of existence." You spurn the teaching about an appointed place of eternal punishment called Hell and insist that Hell is merely the grave. Since man is earth oriented, Heaven is not the hope of most humans. However, Jehovah in his sovereignty has elected 144,000 humans, also called "the Church" and "the little flock," and will cause them to be resurrected as spirit creatures just as Christ was. They alone of all humans will "be born again," will live with God in Heaven and will share in His heavenly service.

You also insist that faithful Witnesses of the Theocracy, called "the other sheep," will escape Armageddon to enjoy the bliss of the earthly millennial paradise. And *if* they carry out Jehovah's righteous laws, they will never die again, you say. Representatives of "the other sheep" who died sometime in the interval since the time of Christ will be raised to a similar opportunity by continuing obedience rewarded by everlasting life. Faithful men of old who lived before the time of Christ will be raised as princely leaders in the government of the new earth under King Jesus and the 144,000.

In utter contrast to these favored groups are "the goats," whom you regard as those people of all nations who rejected or ignored the Kingdom message preached by you Jehovah's Witnesses. These rejecting ones living in the last times will be destroyed in the battle of Armageddon. Though theoretically all the dead are to be given a second chance for restoration, those non-believing "goats" not ransomed by Jesus are destined for external destruction and may not even be raised from the dead. Isn't this what you teach?

At the heart of your Jehovah's Witnesses' teaching is the conflict between Jehovah and the created spirit person, Satan. Satan is held responsible for inventing the doctrines of the trinity, of the immortality of the human soul, of a burning Hell, and of everlasting punishment. He is the originator of all religion and is the murderer of Jesus. All the governments of this world are under his sway, and therefore when individual Witnesses pledge allegiance to an earthly government, they are acknowledging Satan's rule and betraying Jehovah's rightful supremacy.

In the catalogue of end-time events that precede the battle of Armageddon, your Watchtower writers emphasize the termination of Gentile domination in 1914. Because the end of the Gentile times signaled the coming to power of Jehovah's Theocratic government, Satan immediately "sought to swallow up the new-born government," was cast out of Heaven together with His demon hordes and banished to earth. Satan retaliated by plunging the globe into World War I. The nations instigated by the devil, fought furiously to regain their lost earth dominion.

Your writers explain that the far vaster conflict, World War II, was fought by the same opponents for the same reason—world domination. In a further effort to reestablish Gentile world dominance, the nations set up first the League of Nations and then the United Nations. In fact, according to your writers, the U.N. organization is the "abomination of desolation" predicted by Jesus. The ecclesiastically backed governments that masterminded the United Nations constitute the first beast of Revelation 13, while the Anglo-American powers make up the second.

Let's look even further into your teachings. At the present hour, Jehovah is pouring out His wrath on Satan's political-religious system in a period of time described by Christ as the "great tribulation." This will culminate in the climactic battle of Armageddon when Jehovah's Vice-Regent, Jesus, will come as Warrior King and, accompanied by the 144,000, will vanquish the combined armies of earth. Though already "enthroned as King over the earth" in 1914, Christ will not become the reigning global overlord until after Satan, His adversary, is bound. Then He will set up His long awaited millennial kingdom, the New World, the global Paradise.

Let's go on. During the thousand years, the sheep-like survivors of Armageddon, together with the resurrected dead, will be given a second opportunity to merit everlasting life in the earthly Paradise. This will be possible only through strict obedience to Jehovah's requirements contained in special scrolls. As a final test for the millennial law keepers, Satan will be loosed briefly from his prison and will attempt to lead many astray for the final rebellion. Those who maintain their integrity and reject Satan's overtures will be rewarded with everlasting life. All the others will be annihilated together with the devil and his demons.

This brings us to our third question, Why does your group, calling itself the International Bible Students Association, come up with such a vastly different interpretation of the Scriptures than that cherished by people like myself, whom I call fundamental, Bible-believers? The answer seems to be that you Jehovah's Witnesses have devised your own private rules for Biblical interpretation which are basically different from the long established guidelines for sound Biblical exposition. In other words, you are engaged in the same game but are not using the same rules.

Briefly stated, the long established and traditional laws of Bible study are these: 1) The law of *construction* states that the Bible exegete must pay strict attention to the grammar of the original languages and particularly the usage of words throughout the Scriptures. 2) The law of *comprehensiveness* insists that all of the verses on a particular subject must be considered before doctrine is formulated. 3) The law of *comparison* demands that all parallel and related passages must be compared. 4) The law of *context* calls for an intensive examination of the verses that go before and those that follow. 5) The law of *contrast* invites a close consideration of things which superficially appear to be the same but are actually different. 6) The law of *continuity* requires the Bible student to notice God's plan for the ages in every part of the Word. 7) The law of *Christ* views the Lord Jesus Christ as the key to the Scriptures.

In your view, the Bible is a divine drama of Jehovah's vindication. This you believe is the key to understanding the Bible. You see four main characters in this drama: Jehovah, Man, Satan and Christ. Of course, the primary personage is Jehovah whom you claim is a unitary being.

Would you agree to examine some key passages that deal with the Godhead and see what the Scriptures themselves have to say about this crucial subject? As you Witnesses yourselves insist, "Let God be true but every man a liar."[1]

The first verse of the Bible states, "In the beginning God created the heaven and the earth."[2] Using the law of construction, we notice that the Hebrew word for God, "Elohim," is plural and that it is repeated 32 times in this chapter in the plural form. Note also that each time a singular verb follows. What are we to conclude?

Your *New World Translation* note at this point suggests that the plural means "the excellence of majesty." But what proof is there for such an assertion? To the contrary, when Moses, superintended by the Spirit,[3] chose a plural name for God when he could have easily used the singular, he was suggesting a multiple personality. This impression is reinforced by the declaration made by God in this same chapter, "Let us make man in our image after our likeness."[4]

One of your Watchtower writers, admits that God is addressing Jesus here but tries to blunt the evident plural personality of the Godhead by saying that God and His spirit creature Jesus together created Adam. The fatal weakness of this assertion is the fact that God is solitary creator in Genesis one. A created co-creator is not even hinted at, but a person coequal with God and face to face with God is definitely portrayed.[5] Granted, this does not in itself prove a Trinity but it does show that God is more than a solitary person.

A classic verse on the Godhead is the famous "Shema" of Deuteronomy six, which states, "The LORD [Jehovah] our God [Elohim] is one LORD [Jehovah]."[6] The word for "one" in this great declaration is not "yachid" which means "absolute mathematical oneness" but rather "echad" which means the "united one." This definition of the word "echad" is verified graphically in Genesis one where evening and morning make up one day.[7] Also, in the description of the first marriage, a man and his wife are called one flesh.[8] In both cases, two separate entities are considered one.

This Biblical teaching of a plurality of persons in the Godhead is further demonstrated by the fact that Jesus Christ is called Jehovah or equated with Jehovah in a number of parallel key passages.

Isaiah affirmed that "the LORD [Jehovah] shall be unto thee an everlasting light, and thy God thy glory."[9] The aged Simeon, while holding the infant Jesus in his arms, emphasized these same two attributes which belong to Jehovah alone when he declared that this child would grow up to be "a light to lighten the Gentiles, and the glory of thy people Israel."[10]

At the time of his temple vision, Isaiah saw the glory of Jehovah.[11] The Apostle John in referring to Christ says that Isaiah actually saw the glory of Jesus and spoke of Him.[12]

Both David and Isaiah confessed Jehovah to be the personal shepherd for the believing one.[13] Jesus Himself says that He is the shepherd of the sheep.[14]

The Old Testament Scriptures are abundantly clear that Jehovah alone forgives sin[15] and yet Jesus personally forgave the sins of the poor paralytic.[16]

Only Jehovah is worthy of worship and idolaters will surely be punished.[17] Yet the Lord Jesus willingly allowed Thomas to worship Him as his personal Lord and God.[18]

The Apostle Paul cites the promise of Joel that "whosoever shall call on the name of the LORD [Jehovah] shall be delivered"[19] and applies it directly to the salvation of the sinner who calls on the name of Jesus.[20]

Not only is Jesus Christ equated with Jehovah in the absolute sense, but the Holy Spirit is also called Jehovah. For instance, the Jehovah Adonai who commissioned Isaiah[21] is called the Holy Spirit by Paul when he quotes the passage at length.[22] Further, the New Covenant promised by Jehovah in Jeremiah[23] is attributed to the Holy Spirit by the writer of Hebrews.[24] A similar instance is the revelation made in the opening verse of Hebrews[25] that God inspired the prophets. Peter unequivocally asserts that prophetic inspiration came by the Holy Spirit.[26]

The foregoing verses and many more show beyond the shadow of a doubt that Jehovah is a unity of persons and not a solitary being, as you Witnesses claim. The Scriptures reveal that the unity of persons is in fact threefold. Theologically, this Bible doctrine has been termed the "Trinity."

A classic passage of Scripture which undisputedly names the three persons of the Godhead is found in Matthew 28. In what has been called the Magna Charta of the Church, the risen Jesus commanded His followers to go and make disciples of all nations, "baptizing them in the name of the Father, and of the Son, and the Holy Ghost."[27] Notice, that the baptizing is to be done in the *name* (singular) of the threefold God. This is demonstrated even more clearly by the fact that each name has the definite article "the" and not just that of the Father. Significantly, your most popular Jehovah's Witness manuals which question the Trinity invariably omit this verse in Matthew as well as Paul's trinitarian benediction in II Corinthians 13.[28]

Regrettably too, your Watchtower writers have distorted the facts of history by suggesting, for instance, that the supposed twin "trinities" of the Babylonians proves a pagan origin of the trinitarian doctrine. However, these so-called trinities were merely considered leading gods in a pantheon of over 4000 gods. If the germinal suggestion of a trinity is present in Babylon, it more likely suggests a much corrupted Biblical teaching just as the garbled Babylonian account of Noah's flood points to the uncorrupted Biblical account.

When it comes to the teaching about the person of Jehovah, let us not imagine, as one of your writers has done, that only gray-haired professors in ivy covered offices still believe and teach the doctrine of the Trinity. As a matter of fact, all born-again believers assert it as a cornerstone of the Christian faith.

[1] Romans 3:4
[2] Genesis 1:1
[3] II Peter 1:21
[4] Genesis 1:26
[5] John 1:1
[6] Deuteronomy 6:4
[7] Genesis 1:5
[8] Genesis 2:24
[9] Isaiah 60:19
[10] Luke 2:32
[11] Isaiah 6:1,3,5
[12] John 12:37,41
[13] Psalm 23:1; Isaiah 40:10,11
[14] John 10:11
[15] Psalm 130:3,4; Isaiah 43:25; 44:22; Daniel 9:9; Micah 7:17,18
[16] Mark 2:5-12
[17] Exodus 20:2-5; 24:1; 34:14; Deuteronomy 16:10; I Samuel 1:3,19
[18] John 20:28,29
[19] Joel 2:32
[20] Romans 10:9,10,13
[21] Isaiah 6:9,10
[22] Acts 28:25-27
[23] Jeremiah 31:31-34
[24] Hebrews 10:15-17
[25] Hebrews 1:1
[26] II Peter 1:21
[27] Matthew 28:19
[28] II Corinthians 13:14

Man -- Eternal or Temporal?

As you and I already know, man is one of the four important personages in the divine drama of Jehovah's vindication. Because of this, it is imperative that both of us know exactly what the Bible teaches about man. According to your official teaching, "a human is a soul. He does not possess a soul separate and distinct from the body." It is true that the Hebrew word for soul, "nephesh," often does have this meaning. However, the word sometimes designates the immaterial, invisible life principle of man in distinction from his body. An excellent example is that of Elijah as he cries out to Jehovah in behalf of the widow's dead son. Elijah prayed,

"Let this child's soul come into him again,"[1] or to state it more literally, "Let this child's life return upon his inward part." In answer to this impassioned prayer, "the soul of the child came into him again, and he revived [came back to life]."[2]

The definite distinction between soul and body is brought out far more clearly by the New Testament Greek word *psuchee*. In a solemn warning to His disciples, the Lord Jesus cautions, "And fear not them which kill the body, but are not able to kill the soul: but rather fear Him which is able to destroy both soul and body in hell [gehenna].[3] Peter in his Pentecost sermon teaches this same dichotomy between soul and body when, citing Psalm 16,[4] he quotes the words of Messiah, "Because thou wilt not leave my soul in hell [hades], neither wilt thou suffer thine Holy One to see corruption."[5] Paul also makes the same distinction when he lifts up the lifeless body of Eutychus and declares, "Trouble not yourselves, for his life [soul] is in him."[6]

If you will search for yourself, using the law of comprehensiveness, you will discover numerous other verses that pinpoint the Bible truth that man not only is a soul but has a soul which is separated from the body at death.[7]

By the way, have you ever really studied what the Scriptures have to say about "death"? Your little book on doctrine, *Make Sure of All Things* defines death as "loss of life: termination of existence, utter cessation of conscious, intellectual or physical activity, celestial, human or otherwise." This definition assumes that man is merely a physical being and that consequently, death is mere physical death.

What about Adam? Before the Fall, Jehovah Elohim warned the first man that "in the day" that he ate of the forbidden fruit he would "surely die."[8] H.C. Leupold, an acknowledged Hebrew scholar translates it, "in the day of thy eating of it, thou shalt certainly die." Your own translation is similar. In what sense then did Adam and his wife die on the day of their sinning?

Your leaders teach that the soul is inseparable from man and that the spirit of man is his breath. Logically then, the only way that Adam could have died at that particular moment was physically. However, the Scripture is plain that the first man lived physically many hundreds of years after the first sin.[9]

In contrast, if you understand that soul and spirit are the non-physical aspects of the human nature, it is easy to see that Adam died spiritually at the moment he sinned. The Bible says that Adam passed this spiritual death along to every member of the human race.[10] Thus, every person, before he is made spiritually alive by personal faith in Christ, is "dead in trespasses and sins."[11] Eventually, as in Adam's experience, physical death also comes upon the members of his race[12] but this is not the "termination of existence" as your Bible study manual suggests.

In fact, a real blind spot, it would seem, in your Witness teaching is a failure to face the fact of eternal death.

If eternal death is indeed Scriptural, then eternal punishment in a place called hell (gehenna) is more than just a false conception of "apostate Christianity."

According to the teaching of Peter, after Judas the betrayer committed suicide he went "to his own place."[13] As Richard Lenski expresses it, "His own place means of course, the one and only one befitting him." In no sense can this statement be construed to mean "termination of existence." Again, Jesus speaks plainly about the rich man who, after his burial, experienced torment in a place called hell (hades).[14] If this passage is merely symbolical as your teachers insist, then hades, the reality, must be far more appalling than literal fire and parched tongues. Remember, the symbol is always a partial and lesser representation of the reality. Who would be prepared to say that the reality here is annihilation?

In II Thessalonians, Paul reveals that at His glorious revelation from Heaven, Jesus will take full vengeance in flaming fire "on them that know not God, and that obey not the gospel."[15] He declares that these God and Christ rejectors "shall be punished with everlasting [eternal] destruction from the presence [face] of the Lord and from the glory of his power."[16] Notice that the divine penalty which will be meted out to the willfully disobedient is called "eternal destruction." The Greek word translated interchangeably eternal and everlasting is *aioonios*. In three cases the word describes undefined duration and in the remaining 68 examples means endless duration. This is plainly demonstrated by the fact that the word is used of God Himself,[17] of God's power,[18] of God's glory,[19] of Christ's redemptive work,[20] and of the life received by those who personally trust Christ as Saviour.[21] Don't you agree that the openhearted observer ought to conclude that the same word that defines God, Christ and redemption as of endless duration also describes Jehovah's punishment for the unbelieving wicked as of endless duration?

This conclusion is greatly reinforced by a careful consideration of the Greek word *olethros* translated "destruction" in this passage. In the words of W.E. Vine, the noted Greek expert, "This word like its synonyms, also translated 'destroy,' 'destruction,' means, not the destruction of being but of well-being, not annihilation, the putting an end to the existence of a person or thing, but its ruin so far as the purpose of its existence is concerned."

In Revelation 14, a judgment angel announces solemnly that anyone who worships the future antichrist and his image, or who receives his mark on the forehead or on the hand "shall drink of the [unmixed] wine of the wrath [vehement fury] of God, which is poured out without mixture [undiluted] into the cup of his indignation [settled wrath]."[22] Three closely connected things characterize this pouring out of God's fury upon these rebellious humans: 1) They shall individually be tormented by (in) fire and brimstone (sulfur) before the holy angels and before Jesus the Lamb.[23] How significant that in 12 of the 19 times in which judgment fires are mentioned in the New Testament, it is the Lord Jesus who uses the word "fire." 2) The "smoke of their torment" (this sounds like real fire) keeps on ascending up unto the ages of the ages (eternally).[24] 3) They will not have rest day and night because of the intensity of the heat and the density of the smoke.[25]

In Revelation 20, the unregenerate dead are cast (hurled) into the lake of fire which is defined as "the second death."[26] Obviously, the resurrected bodies of these wicked dead will not burn instantly as a match burns paper but will continue to burn forever. This is demonstrated by the fact that the beast and his false prophet will be cast bodily into the lake of fire burning with brimstone before the millennial reign of Christ.[27] A thousand years later, Satan will join his two former confederates when he, too, will be cast into the lake of fire and brimstone. Jointly, the three "shall be tormented day and night forever and ever [eternally]."[28] These two verses show clearly that the infamous human duo not only bodily survive a millennium in the lake of fire but that their suffering will continue perpetually.

But I am sure that you must be protesting, "What about the meaning of sheol, hades and gehenna? Is it not true that sheol in the Old Testament and hades in the New Testament means "the grave," "gravedom" and "nonexistence in the land of the dead"?

As Girdlestone in his classic work, *Synonyms of the Old Testament* so ably shows, the Hebrew word "sheol" often does mean the grave, the place of the dead. On the other hand, a number of other passages speak of "sheol" as the place which is located in the opposite direction from Heaven where darkness and silence reign and where none can praise Jehovah.

Job declares that the depths of God "are as high as heaven . . . deeper than hell [sheol]."[29] David asserts, "If I ascend up into heaven, thou are there:

If I make my bed in hell [sheol], behold thou art there."[30] Isaiah prophesies concerning the fallen Lucifer, "Yet thou shalt be brought down to hell [sheol], to the sides [farthest recesses] of the pit."[31] Amos quoting Jehovah says, "Though they dig into hell [sheol], thence shall mine hand take them; though they climb up to heaven, thence will I bring them down."[32] Jonah says, "I cried by reason of mine affliction unto the LORD [Jehovah] and he heard me; out of the belly [womb] of hell [sheol] I cried and thou heardest my voice."[33] The citations could continue. However, these are sufficient to show that "sheol" in relation to the dead is more than mere "unconscious annihilation in dust of the ground."

Notice, that all these examples come before the Babylonian exile. Bible students have noticed that during the exile, God greatly expanded His revelation concerning Satan, angels and particularly about the afterlife. Thus, the prophet Daniel definitely speaks of a bodily resurrection of both just and unjust with eternal consequences when he predicts, "And many of them that sleep in the dust of the earth shall awake, some to everlasting life, and some to shame [disgrace] and everlasting contempt [lit. abhorrence]."[34]

To this exilic promise of future resurrection bliss for the righteous and conscious pain and remorse for the wicked, the Lord Jesus adds the further revelation that immediately at death the soul of the redeemed one goes to a place of immediate happiness, called by Him, "Abraham's bosom"[35] and "paradise"[36] while the unredeemed man goes to hell [hades].[37] Certainly, hades cannot be the grave for the rich man in this eyewitness account in Luke 16 sees, feels, cries, remembers and prays.[38] In the only four instances where the word "hades" is used in the Gospels, Jesus uses it Himself.

You may have been asking about "gehenna." A close study of the usage of this word reveals that "gehenna" and the lake of fire, already discussed, are synonymous. Your teachers also believe this, with the important difference, of course, that they insist that "conscious eternal torment (is) not in the Scriptures but Eternal Destruction is, symbolized by Gehenna and 'Lake of Fire.' "

Notice, again, that the Lord Jesus uses "gehenna" 11 of the 12 times the word is found in the New Testament. Without doubt, Jesus is the acknowledged expert on the subject of the fate of the wicked! In His Sermon on the Mount, Christ warns, "Whosoever shall say, Thou fool [empty-headed idiot], shall be in danger of hell [gehenna] fire."[39] Again, he sounds the alarm by insisting that if the individual's right eye or right hand cause him to stumble, he would be better off destroying it rather than that the "whole body should be cast into hell [gehenna]."[40] At a later time, when the Saviour repeats these same warnings about offending eyes and hands, He adds the foot as well. Note that in the first passage,[41] Jesus speaks of the individual (you) as in danger of being "cast into everlasting fire," and in the companion verse, He warns against the person (you) being "cast into hellfire," literally, the "hell (gehenna) of fire."[42]

That this is a place of eternal torment is amply demonstrated by the parallel passage in Mark 9,[43] where Christ three times describes "gehenna" as the place of unquenchable (literally, asbestos) fire. To this He adds the frightening thrice-repeated description, "where their worm dieth not."

The comment of A. T. Robertson, the unimpeachable Greek scholar, on these verses is illuminating. He says, "The valley of Hinnon (gehenna) had been desecrated by the sacrifice of children to Moloch so that as an accursed place it was used for the city garbage where worms gnawed and fires burned. It is thus a vivid picture of eternal punishment."

In Luke 12, Jesus warns His disciples that they are not to fear men who, after all, can only kill the body, but they ought to be in awe of God who "after he has killed hath power [authority] to cast into hell [gehenna]."[44] To this, the Redeemer adds, "Fear him [God] which is able to destroy [cause to lose well-being] both body and soul in hell [gehenna]."[45]

The last recorded time Christ uses the word "gehenna" is in His castigation of the hypocritical Scribes and Pharisees. He calls them serpents and vipers and then asks, "How can ye escape the damnation [judgment] of hell [gehenna]?"[46]

Again, I invite you to search the Scriptures for yourself using one of the larger concordances suggested. Bear in mind the context, apply the law of comprehensiveness and notice the gradual unfolding of this Bible doctrine with its full culmination in the New Testament. After completing my personal study of "sheol," "hades" and "gehenna" I am convinced that the Word of God suggests a broader definition of eternal death than mere termination of existence. Death in a Biblical sense is, rather, a separation of the unregenerate man in every part of his nature from the life of God. This involves the dissolution of the body in the grave, the fiery torment of the soul in hades and the final casting of the resurrected individual (body, soul and spirit) into the everlasting punishment of the lake of fire (gehenna) which is also called "the second death."

From a personal investigation of the Scriptures some 25 years ago, I came to the glad conclusion that the heart of the Bible's teaching is God's demonstrated concern for the personal salvation of lost individuals. For this reason, God gave as a sacrifice His only begotten Son that whosoever (literally, anyone) believing in Him should not perish (lose well-being) but have as a present possession ever-continuing, undestroyable life.[47] Further, "He that believeth on him [Christ] is not condemned [judged]: but he that believeth not is condemned already, because he has not believed in the name of the only begotten Son of God."[48] John expresses it this way, "He that hath [present tense] the Son hath life; and he that hath not the Son of God hath not life."[49] Paul bears testimony to his personal salvation by affirming, "For to me to live is Christ. . . ."⁵⁰ Peter in writing to the scattered Jewish Christians of Asia Minor declares, "Forasmuch as ye know that ye were not redeemed with corruptible things, as silver and gold, from your vain conversation [manner of living] received by tradition from your fathers; but with the precious blood of Christ, as of a lamb without blemish and without spot."⁵¹

It was a transforming day when I discovered that salvation in Christ is personal and immediately available but better still that it is a free gift from God. I read in the second chapter of Ephesians, "For by grace [free gift] are ye saved through faith; and that not of yourselves [as a source]: it is the gift of God: not of works lest any man should boast. For we are his workmanship, created in [union with] Christ Jesus unto good works. . . ."⁵² Again, I read in the book of Romans, "Being [present tense] justified [acquitted] freely [gratis] by his grace [free gift] through the redemption that is in Christ Jesus: Whom God hath set [put] forth to be a propitiation [a satisfaction] through faith in his blood. . . ."[53] It slowly dawned on my consciousness that the free gift of personal, immediate salvation from God cannot be earned or worked for any more than a free gift from man can be earned.

Salvation, then, is not of my works, struggles, attempts, sincere devotion, religious activity, doing one's best. Salvation is God's free gift to me for the asking (faith).[54] Further, salvation is not just for a limited few but for all who call upon the name of the Lord Jesus, asking for His provided salvation.[55]

When the Spirit of God made all of this new truth real to my heart, I bowed my head on my college desk and confessed that I was a mere religionist lost in my sins. I thanked the LORD for sending His Son to suffer personally for my personal sins on Calvary.[56] Then, as a free gift I received the Lord Jesus Christ as my personal Saviour from sin. In that moment, He made me a new creature. The old life and the old ways passed away and all things became new to me.⁵⁷ As a new-born baby in Christ, I intensely and recurringly desired the nourishing milk of the Word.⁵⁸ I have not the slightest shadow of doubt that on that January day when I trusted the Saviour, I was begotten (born) again spiritually⁵⁹ and became a child of God.⁶⁰

Through the years, I have been mystified as to why this personally and immediately possessed salvation by grace seems to be totally lacking in your Jehovah's Witnesses' teaching. Then I read a statement from one of your Brooklyn Superintendents in which he suggested that an emphasis on "soul salvation" and "God's vindication" are mutually exclusive. He illustrated this by the Lord's prayer. He said that the prayer "starts out asking that our Father's name be sanctified, His Kingdom installed over the earth, His righteousness established. It ends up asking for our personal daily welfare and salvation." He summarized by saying that "if the principal theme is soul salvation, only the latter part of the prayer will stand out" but "if the main theme is the vindication of God's name and truth and purposes" a vastly different viewpoint will be derived by the same prayer.

Let me reply at once, that I personally emphasize the so-great-salvation that the Bible emphasizes but together with tens of thousands of fundamental, Bible-believing pre-millennial Christians I believe that God will literally rule upon this earth through His beloved Son and that God's name will be vindicated by the defeat of Satan, of false religion and of the Satanically controlled world-system. I believe that this is an integral part of God's redemptive plan.

Again, you are no doubt wondering how it is possible for two groups of Bible students, the Jehovah's Witnesses and the pre-millennial Christians, both of whom uphold the importance of God's vindication, to end up by holding such divergent views.

The answer seems to lie in a basic key to Bible interpretation about man. I have nowhere found this in your Witness teaching. It is the foundational truth that we need always to distinguish God's plan and work for: 1) the Jew, 2) the Gentile and 3) the church.⁶¹

As you know, your official publications teach that the Jews as a race and as a nation have been cast off forever because of the rejection of Jesus by the Jewish mob in Jerusalem just prior to His crucifixion.⁶² Thus, according to your teachings, every promise made to the "natural Jews" of Abraham's race has been transferred since the day of Pentecost to the "new nation" of spiritual Israel which is composed of both Jews and Gentiles. Consequently, the physical people of Abraham's seed, the Jews, will never be restored to Palestine by Jehovah as He once promised because He has cast them off as His chosen people. As one of your Witness writers has put it, "The facts and prophecies prove that the natural Jew will never again be a chosen, regathered people. They have as a people flagrantly rejected the Messiah, his truth and his kingdom." This, by the way, is just the opposite of what your founder, Pastor Charles Russell taught in his book *The Time Is At Hand*.

Is it Scriptural, then, to say that Jehovah has cast off earthly Israel forever? If not, what is Israel's present and prospective position in the divine plan of world redemption? To begin with, we need to understand that God's basic covenant with Abraham, unconditionally promises Abraham a chosen pattern—spiritual blessing to the nations,[63] a chosen place—the land of Israel[64] and a chosen people—Abraham's physical seed.[65] The covenant sign which Jehovah requires of the Jewish race is physical circumcision,[66] the one practice which has been zealously kept since the days of Moses. Because the Abrahamic covenant is based on the immutable "I will" of God[67] it is also an "everlasting covenant"[68] which cannot, therefore, be terminated by the all-too-prevalent rebellion of the Jewish people.

It is true that because of Israel's national defiance, Hosea warns, "The children of Israel shall abide many days without a king, and without a prince, and without a [slain] sacrifice, and without an image [pillar], and without an ephod, and without teraphim. . . ."[69] But this does not mean that God is finished with the Jewish nation. For the next verse says, "Afterward, shall the children of Israel return, and seek the LORD [Jehovah] their God, and David their king; and shall fear the LORD and his goodness in the latter years."[70]

Couple this with Ezekiel's parallel promise, "I will make them [Israel and Judah] one nation in the land upon the mountains of Israel; and one king shall be king to them all. . . .[71] I will save them out of all their dwelling places, wherein they have sinned, and will cleanse them: so shall they be my people, and I will be their God. . . . And they shall dwell in the land that I have given unto Jacob my servant . . . . forever: and my servant David shall be their prince forever."[72]

The relationship between the scattered Jews and the dominant Gentile world powers in this present age and unto the glorious appearing of King Jesus, is demonstrated by the prediction of Christ Himself. He states, "And they [the Jewish people] shall fall by the edge of the sword, and shall be led away captive into all nations: and Jerusalem shall be trodden down of the Gentiles, until the times [period] of the Gentiles be fulfilled [runs its course]."[73]

The contrast between Israel and the church is maintained by the Apostle Paul in the epistle to the Romans. After charging the Jewish people with rebellion and disobedience to God,[74] Paul asks the all important question, "Hath God cast away [repudiated] his people?" His answer is swift and emphatic, "God forbid."[75] He then goes on to show that through Israel's stumbling, God has brought salvation to the Gentiles who make up a greater part of the Church.[76] He continues, "Now if the diminishing of them

[Jews] be the riches of the Gentiles; how much more their fullness?"[77] Then, in a decisive summarizing statement addressed to the believers (the church), he affirms "blindness in part is happened to Israel, until the fullness of the Gentiles be come in. And so all Israel shall be saved."[78]

Undeniably then, Jehovah has a plan that includes the three classifications of mankind: the Jew, Gentile and Church.

[1] I Kings 17:21
[2] I Kings 17:22
[3] Matthew 10:28; cf. Matthew 6:25
[4] Psalm 16:10
[5] Acts 2:27
[6] Acts 20:10
[7] Luke 12:20
[8] Genesis 2:17
[9] Genesis 5:3-5
[10] Romans 5:12,15-17
[11] Ephesians 2:1,13
[12] Genesis, chapter 5
[13] Acts 1:25
[14] Luke 16:22-24
[15] II Thessalonians 1:7,8
[16] II Thessalonians 1:9
[17] Romans 16:26
[18] I Timothy 6:16
[19] I Peter 5:10
[20] Hebrews 9:12
[21] John 3:16
[22] Revelation 14:9-11
[23] Revelation 14:10
[24] Revelation 14:11a
[25] Revelation 14:11b
[26] Revelation 20:11-15
[27] Revelation 19:20
[28] Revelation 20:10
[29] Job 11:8
[30] Psalm 139:8
[31] Isaiah 14:15
[32] Amos 9:2
[33] Jonah 2:2
[34] Daniel 12:2
[35] Luke 16:22
[36] Luke 23:43
[37] Luke 16:23
[38] Luke 16:23-31
[39] Matthew 5:22
[40] Matthew 5:29,30
[41] Matthew 18:8
[42] Matthew 18:9
[43] Mark 9:43-47
[44] Luke 12:4,5
[45] Matthew 10:28

[46] Matthew 23:33
[47] John 3:16
[48] John 3:18
[49] I John 5:12
[50] Philippians 1:21
[51] I Peter 1:18,19
[52] Ephesians 2:8, 9; cf. 2:5
[53] Romans 3:24,25
[54] John 1:12; Romans 10:9, 10
[55] Romans 10:13
[56] II Corinthians 5:21
[57] II Corinthians 5:17
[58] I Peter 2:2
[59] John 3:3,5; I Peter 1:1-3
[60] Galatians 3:26; 4:6; I John 3:1,2
[61] I Corinthians 10:32
[62] Matthew 27:25
[63] **Genesis 12:2,3;** 22:17,18
[64] Genesis 13:15.17; 15:7,8,18; 17:8
[65] **Genesis 12:7; 13:15,** 16; 15:5,18; 17:2,4-6; 22:17
[66] Genesis 17:13
[67] Genesis 12:3,7; 13:15
[68] Genesis 17:7,8
[69] Hosea 3:4
[70] Hosea 3:5
[71] Ezekiel 37:21,22
[72] Ezekiel 37:23-26; cf. 37:27,28
[73] Luke 21:24
[74] Romans 10:21
[75] Romans 11:1
[76] Romans 11:11
[77] Romans 11:12
[78] Romans 11:25,26

Satan -- Presently Cast Down or Prospectively Cast Down?

Another character in the drama of Jehovah's Vindication is the evil personality called Satan. Unlike the liberals and skeptics, you believe, as the Bible teaches, that Satan is a fallen angel who is responsible for the temptation of our first parents. He is a murderer and incites the evil deeds of both demons and lost men. He is the god of this evil world-system and is in open conflict with Christ.

However, three dated statements in one of your books, *Make Sure of All*

Things, cause me great perplexity. In the first of these, your writer asserts that Satan became god of the world "in the broadest sense in 607 B.C. at the time of the fall of Jehovah's Typical Theocratic Government at Jerusalem." A quick look in your chart of dates printed in *Babylon the Great Has Fallen* reveals that in 607 B.C. the temple was razed and Jerusalem was destroyed. Upon what evidence does this chronological chart rest? Every reputable Bible Dictionary I have consulted gives the date for the fall of Jerusalem as 587-586 B.C. Edwin R. Thiele, who has probably done more work on the dating of the kings of Israel and Judah than anyone else, lists 586 B.C. as the actual date.

A mere date may seem like a small matter except that 607 B.C. is crucial to the chronology of the second statement. This declares that "Satan's uninterrupted rule of the nations extended '7 Times' (2520 years) till his failure to overcome the newborn Kingdom in Heaven, A.D. 1914." It is obvious that the author of this summary believes that the expression "times" means "years of days." Thus, by multiplying 7 by the 360 days in the Hebrew sacred year, the result is 2520. Then, by adding the 607 years B.C. to the A.D. 1914 years (exclusive of the terminal years), the result is 2520 years. This sounds very impressive, except for some disturbing facts: 1) no one else equates the 607 B.C. date with Jerusalem's destruction. The historically attested date is some 20 years later, which would bring the terminal date to 1934, a year of worldwide depression not of world war. 2) The passage in Daniel 4 where the expression "times" is found,[1] does not refer to Satan at all but to an actual king, Nebuchadnezzar, whom God punished with madness for seven years because of his overweening pride. 3) When applied to King Nebuchadnezzar, the expression "times" could not mean years of 360 days. Obviously, he did not live until 1914 or 1934 since Daniel names one of his successors in the next chapter.[2]

In connection with the year 1914, I

notice that your leaders affirm that in that year Satan failed to overthrow the newly established Kingdom of Christ in Heaven. Frankly, I am mystified about the reference to Jesus being invisibly crowned King of the new world in Heaven in 1914. The Saviour in speaking to His disciples promises, "And if I go and prepare a place for you, I will come again and receive you [take you along] unto myself; that where I am, there ye may be also."[3] Again, the angels guarantee the beholding ones of the ascension that "this same Jesus which is taken up from you into heaven, shall so come in like manner [in the same way] as ye have seen him go into heaven."[4] In these two verses believers are assured that the visible Christ will return visibly to His visibly waiting friends.

In answer to this, your writers point out that the Greek word *parousia*, translated "coming" four times in Matthew 24,[5] should rather be rendered "presence" or "arrival," as some translators have rendered it. They insist that "presence" "does not mean that he is on the way, or has promised to come, but that he has already arrived and is present." This apparently proves that Jesus is already enthroned in Heaven invisibly and that **the promise of** His public enthronement in earthly Jerusalem is a mistake.[6] However, if you will take the time to examine the word *parousia* in one of the concordances already suggested, you will discover that the word always suggests visible bodily presence even in passages which make no reference to the return of the Redeemer.[7]

Apparently, the primary importance of referring to the word *parousia* in Matthew 24 is the fact that in that particular discourse Christ predicts that before His coming (presence) "nation shall rise against nation, and kingdom against kingdom. . . ."[8] Your Jehovah's Witness leaders have taken this to be an infallible reference to the beginning of World War I in 1914. The persecution and affliction of Christ's true followers that Jesus next predicts is taken to mean the ridicule, opposition and imprisonment of the Kingdom Publishers in the period from 1914-1918.[9] The warning of the Saviour about the distrust and betrayal that will mar the believers' fellowship in those days,[10] is taken to mean the split within your Jehovah's Witness ranks which resulted in a renewed organization of Kingdom Publishers under President J. F. Rutherford.

Again, the apparent lineup of events is impressive but too much depends on the pinpointing of the very general war references to a particular conflict —World War I. Did you know that a similar lineup of events also characterized the Thirty Years War? The final result was the publishing of the Good News by the Pietists. However, neither at that time, nor in World War I did the Abomination of Desolation (the personal antichrist) stand in the holy place of a rebuilt Jerusalem Jewish temple demanding worship.[11]

Of course, your leaders deny a future for the Jews and therefore identify "the abomination that maketh desolate" with the League of Nations, later the United Nations. It must be as apparent to you as it is to me that your Watchtower interpretation is highly spiritualized. Personally, I would never have dreamed that the Abomination of Desolation is the League of Nations if I had not read it first in one of your Jehovah's Witness publications.

The third troubling statement concerning Satan in your little book of doctrine is vitally connected with what we have just been considering. It affirms that "cast down from Heaven to Earth[12] by the King Christ Jesus, A.D. 1914-1918, Satan's activities are confined to earth." The first thing Satan did when expelled from Heaven, according to one of your writers, was to plunge the nations of earth into the War of 1914-1918. His real purpose was the destruction of "all peoples ere they learned of the newly established kingdom." Aiding him in his diabolic purposes were his two confederates mentioned in Revelation 13. The first of these, the Beast with 10 horns,[13] was identified with the ecclesiastically backed nations that fought. The second two-horned Beast[14] was declared to be the Anglo-American World Power because England and the United States had so much to do with the League of Nations, the so-called Abomination of Desolation.

To say the least, this whole interpretation is non-literal and completely ignores the fact that the two beasts are men,[15] not governments. As we have previously noted, how can governments be cast into the lake of fire, and how can Satan eventually share their suffering? Only the literal interpretation fits all the facts.

[1] Daniel 4:16,25
[2] Daniel 5:1,11,12
[3] John 14:3
[4] Acts 1:11
[5] Matthew 24:3,27,37,39
[6] Matthew 24:30,31; 25:31,32; 26:64
[7] II Peter 1:16
[8] Matthew 24:7
[9] Matthew 24:9
[10] Matthew 24:10-12
[11] Matthew 24:15
[12] Revelation 12:7-10
[13] Revelation 13:1-9
[14] Revelation 13:10-17
[15] Revelation 13:18

Jesus--Deity or Deputy?

The fourth major actor in the drama of Jehovah's Vindication is the Lord Jesus Christ. According to your teaching, Jesus "is a created individual, . . . the second greatest Personage of the Universe. . . . He was formed countless millenniums ago, as the first and the only direct creation by his Father, Jehovah, and, because of his proved, faultless integrity, was appointed by Jehovah as His Vindicator and the chief Agent of life toward mankind." Several of your leaders proudly admit that this is Arian teaching.

All of this seems so strange to me since the absolute deity of Christ seems so plainly taught in Scripture. For instance, John teaches the deity of Jesus when in his Gospel he writes,

"In the beginning was the Word [Jesus] and the Word was with [face to face] God and the Word was God."[1] Immediately, you will remember that your own *New World Translation*, following the *Emphatic Diaglott*, translates, "the Word was a god," meaning, as the footnote says, "in contrast with 'the God.'"

The reasoning seems to be that since the Greek word "God" (*theos*) does not have the definite article, it must be translated indefinitely as "a god." This, however, overlooks a very important Greek rule known as Colwell's rule which states, "The absence of the article does not make the predicate indefinite or qualitative when it precedes the verb." In contrast, when the predicate noun comes after the verb, the definite article must be used to make the noun definite. Even a casual look at the Greek text in John 1 shows that the predicate "God" precedes the verb "was" and consequently the testimony of John is that "the Word was God." Incidentally, the literal translation that accompanies the

Greek text in the *Emphatic Diaglott* also bears witness to the fact that "the Logos (Word) was God."

The testimony of the hard-to-convince Thomas concerning the deity of Jesus is just as ringing. When he sees, hears and touches the risen Christ, he cries out in believing worship, "My Lord [emphatic] and my God [emphatic]." Your own translation is nearly identical here.[2]

Paul repeatedly refers to the deity of Christ. In writing to the Philippians, he admonishes them to cultivate the mind of Christ "who being [from the beginning and still continuing] in the form [nature, character, essence] of God, thought it not robbery [a treasure to be grasped at] to be equal with God [God's equal]."[3]

Your *New World Translation* completely changes the thought of the Greek text by saying that Jesus, though "existing in God's form, gave no consideration to a seizure, namely that he should be equal to God."

Joseph Thayer, whom your writers often quote, takes strong exception to such a translation when he interprets, "although he bore the form of God, yet did not think that this equality with God was to be eagerly clung to or retained."

When writing to the Colossians, who were teaching that Jesus is only a creature of God, Paul triumphantly proclaims, "For in him [Jesus] dwelleth [permanently] all the fulness [plenitude] of the Godhead [Deity] bodily [in bodily manifestation]."[4] Notice that the marginal reading of your own translation is strikingly similar, "Because it is in him that all the fullness of the divine quality dwells bodily." This can mean only that Jesus Christ is God.

The Apostle Peter begins his second epistle by rejoicing in the salvation which has been made personally available "through the righteousness of God and our Saviour Jesus Christ."[5] Your translators take this to mean that Peter is distinguishing between the righteousness of God and that of a distinct person, the Saviour. Such a rendering, however, overlooks another basic Greek rule, known since 1798 as Granville Sharp's rule. Mr. Sharp states that "when the copulative 'and' connects two nouns of the same case, if the article precedes the first noun and is not repeated before the second noun, the latter always refers to the same person that is expressed or described by the first noun." Thus, Peter is exulting in the righteousness of God, who is identical with his Saviour, Jesus Christ. If you check carefully, you will discover that Paul uses this exact construction when he writes to Titus concerning the great God who is the same as his Saviour, Christ Jesus.[6]

I wonder if you are fully aware that Jesus Himself plainly disclosed His own deity? It is utterly amazing how your writers have obscured perfectly plain verses in an all-out attempt to disprove this truth. For instance, Jesus openly declared to the Pharisees, "Before Abraham was [came into existence] I am [absolutely timeless]."[7] The usual Witness answer to this obvious exposition is the fact that the Greek construction here is the "Historic

60

Present" and therefore the correct rendering is, "Before Abraham was, I have been." Seasoned Greek scholars, however, do not concur. Samuel G. Green summarizes the matter well when he states, "In vivid narration the Present is employed of past time (Historic Present)." He then says specifically that this verse does not belong in this category.

As you can see by the violent reaction of the Pharisees,[8] the Saviour here definitely makes a claim to deity. What makes this claim so important is the fact that Jesus solemnly declares, "If ye believe not that I am, ye shall die in your sins."[9]

In John 10, the Lord Jesus makes a claim to be God from a different standpoint altogether. In speaking of the Father's absolute power to keep the redeemed sheep, Jesus adds, "I and my Father are one [in power]."[10] As the Psalmist so aptly says, "Power belongeth unto God."[11] When Jesus, therefore, claims equal power with the Father, He is claiming to be God and not a mere deputy of God.

If Jesus Christ is really God, then your whole Jehovah's Witnesses doctrine of the atonement crumbles. As you know, your literature teaches that the sinless man Jesus "an exact replica of Adam" before he sinned, proved faultlessly obedient to the Father "and for this he was exalted and made the great High Priest to enter into 'heaven itself' and offer the value of his perfect human sacrifice on behalf of 'them that obey.'" As a fitting reward for his faithful course, Christ was "granted immortal life." Not only that, but this immortal life will also be given to a limited number (144,000) of "Christ's Body Members for (their perfect) faithfulness until death." The rest of humanity will be given a chance for everlasting life on this earth during the thousand-year reign of Christ.

I have already told you how one day I realized my sinfulness and by simple heart trust asked the crucified-risen Christ to come into my heart and take away my sins. I did not come to this place of personal decision through a doctrine of "equivalent obedience" but rather through the plain Bible teaching of Christ's personal substitution for my sins. My heart welled up in gratitude when I learned that Jesus "was wounded [pierced through] for our transgressions, he was bruised [crushed] for our iniquities: the chastisement [punishment] of [leading to] our peace was upon him, and with his stripes we are healed. All we like sheep have gone astray [scattered]; we have turned every one to his own way; and the LORD [Jehovah] hath laid on him [Christ] the iniquity of us all."[12]

I turned to the New Testament and read, "For he [God] hath made him [Christ] to be sin for us, who knew no sin [was consciously sinless]; that we might be made [may become] the righteousness of God in [in union with] him."[13] I read further that Jesus "his own self bare our sins in his own body on the tree, that [in order that] we being dead to sins, should live unto [for] righteousness: by whose stripes [bruise] ye were healed. For ye were as sheep going astray [wandering]; but are now returned [turned] unto the Shepherd and Bishop [overseer] of your souls."[14]

When I saw the truth that Christ bore my personal sins in His body, I also realized that to die for "us all" He had to be an infinite person. Suddenly, I understood what John meant when he wrote, "And the Word [the eternal Christ] was made [became] flesh [human], and dwelt [tabernacled] among us."[15] In other words, He became the God-Man that I might become a godly man.

Now that I know Christ personally, I am expecting His return eagerly. With the Apostle John, I am praying, "Even so, come Lord Jesus."[16] Do you have this hope too? Make it yours today by trusting in Jesus Christ as your Saviour.

[1] John 1:1
[2] John 20:28
[3] Philippians 2:6
[4] Colossians 2:9
[5] II Peter 1:1
[6] Titus 2:13
[7] John 8:58
[8] John 8:59
[9] John 8:24
[10] John 10:30
[11] Psalm 62:11
[12] Isaiah 53:5,6
[13] II Corinthians 5:21
[14] I Peter 2:24,25
[15] John 1:14
[16] Revelation 22:20